Теперь я очень ... ...
статья очень ...
...венная же для ...
есть Вы без грима: простой и я...
столетие.
Я Вашим разрешением предлагаю
прямо на теле рукописи — хотя в
наглую правку, но так действитель...
раз уж мы не можем поговор...
...ал я внёс двумя цветами: розов...
не, темно-зеленым — менее. Кром...
...пояснял на полях, отчего и по...
ние. Эти последние, чёрные, зам...
евале мелковато, но я рассчит...
...очно будет Люше один раз все...

...мне очень нравится, а чтобы о...
у статьи, добавим ещё „Но сл...
...бочку, это хорошо будет читат...
...ицианнее — через запятую). А
» обязательно маленькими под...
...ами, чтоб не предвзимало. И
...удет после „письмо" поставит...

Ещё я кое-где на полях поставил га[лочки?]
знаки — это особое одобрение лучши[х мест]
по сравнению с письмами к Алигер.
Что ж, не называйте "Нового мира",
зательно напишите! (стр 2, я отм[етил])

На стр 7 я не объяснил главно[го.]
Тут вот что: на абзаце как будто
уверенного выведения из какого-то
тварю. И я предлагаю чуть смя[г]-
чить за Герцена. Цитату из Огар[ё]-
ва тож — ну, а много ли потеряли бы.
А самая последняя на странице — "Г.
- б - тоже облегчить, и от неё?

Для энергии окончания — и там
уменьшить.

Ещё вот что удивительно: объё[м!]
Для такой нагруженной мыслями ста[ть]-
ёй, статья легка! (Но не
[легкомысленна]!)

Испалать же, Лидия Корнеевна
думают! Статья готова, созре[ла?]
умов.

The Writer Who Changed History

ALEKSANDR SOLZHENITSYN

MARGO CAULFIELD
Margo Caulfield 7/26/19

Published in the United States
by the Cavendish Historical Society
Cavendish, Vermont 05142

First U.S. Edition: April 2016
ISBN 978-1530160853

Copyright © 2016 by Cavendish Historical Society.
All rights reseved under the International and Pan-American
Copyright Conventions. For any questions concerning
reprints and permissions, please visit
thewriterwhochangedhistory.com.

Designed by Julia Gignoux, Freedom Hill Design.
Photos courtesy of the Solzhenitsyn family.

CONTENTS

Introduction	A Secret Book Tells a Story	1
Chapter 1	Growing Up During a Civil War	6
	Aleksandr Solzhenitsyn's Russia 7	
	Life Under Stalin 15	
Chapter 2	Arrested	17
Chapter 3	Freedom to Tell the Truth	28
	Major Leaders of the Soviet Union and Russia 34	
Chapter 4	Nobel-Prize Winner	40
Chapter 5	Exiled Again	47
	Why the Soviet Union Was Afraid of Aleksandr 52	
Chapter 6	In the West	58
	The Fall of Communism and the Soviet Union 69	
Chapter 7	Home at Last	73
	Glossary	81
	Timeline	85
	Major Works	88

INTRODUCTION

A SECRET BOOK TELLS A STORY

Imagine yourself in a cramped bathroom, turning pages of a forbidden book as quickly as you can. A friend has passed it to you with a warning, "Read quickly. Keep the book and yourself hidden. Or else." Or else what?

The secret police seem to be everywhere, and their punishments are cruel. You know people who have done next to nothing and have lost their jobs, been dragged to prison, or even disappeared. Disappeared where, you might have wondered?...

And that is why you want to read this book.

a samizdat "cake" book

SAMIZDAT

[**sah**-miz-dot]: Self-published books and papers, made by hand and passed from person to person. Reading these could result in severe punishment from the Soviet government.

Aleksandr Solzhenitsyn is pronounced: [al-ek-**zan**-der sol-zhe-**neet**-sin]

Your eyes strain in the dim light, your body aches, this *samizdat* copy is tattered, but you want to know the truths that courageous Aleksandr Solzhenitsyn tells about the Gulag, a bitter-cold, faraway place from which only rumors escape.

Your cramped bathroom is nothing compared to what Solzhenitsyn describes. *Zeks* (prisoners of the Gulag) live in crowded buildings surrounded by barbed-wire fences.

Biting winds blow through the poorly-insulated walls, and beds are only wooden planks.

typical camp barracks

2

zeks at work

There is not enough warm clothing, or food. Guards beat prisoners for no reason at all, and zeks have been known to fight, or even kill one another, for an extra piece of bread or a warmer jacket.

The work is endless and hard—hauling rocks, cutting down trees, building roads—all usually done by hand. Long exhausting days could end in punishment if guards don't think tasks are completed well enough. An escape attempt could mean instant death by shooting, or starving and freezing in the

GULAG

[**goo**-log]: The Russian abbreviation for Chief Administration of Corrective Labor Camps and Colonies. This was the Soviet Union's vast network of forced-labor camps.

3

a camp watchtower

cold barren lands surrounding the labor camp. Disease and death are common.

From 1918 to 1953, many millions of Russians were taken to these labor camps to work and to die. All this didn't happen that long ago: you might have had a grandparent living during these times. Almost every family lost someone—a father, brother, son, daughter, wife—without warning or explanation. And yet Russians, even today, have barely come to terms with this awful past.

Solzhenitsyn wrote,

> In keeping silent about evil, in burying it so deep within us that no sign of it appears on the surface, we are *implanting* it, and it will rise up a thousandfold in the future.[1]

Would you have taken a risk to read a book that explained everything that your government wanted to hide? What gave Aleksandr Solzhenitsyn the fearless determination to expose the truth?

manuscript of
The Gulag Archipelago

[1] *The Gulag Archipelago*, trans. Thomas P. Whitney, New York: Harper Perennial Modern Classics, 2007, vol. 1, part I, chapter 4, p. 178.

1

GROWING UP DURING A CIVIL WAR

> **WORLD WAR I**
>
> The war between the Triple Alliance and the Central Powers, from 1914 to 1918, that killed at least 30 million people and resulted in a drastic reconfiguration of the world order.

From his birth on December 11, 1918, Aleksandr Solzhenitsyn's mother called him Sanya [**sah**-nya]. In using her husband's nickname, she honored that of Aleksandr's father Isaaki [ee-sah-**ah**-ki], a decorated war hero from World War I, who died in a hunting accident before his son's birth.

Sanya's father

Aleksandr Solzhenitsyn's Russia

Before Sanya's birth, Tsars ruled Russia. Like many kings and queens, Tsars held strong sway over their people. When the Tsar wanted to wage a war, and that happened frequently, the men would have to leave their farms or jobs to go fight. Their being away from family and home meant that farming and other heavy work had to be done by the women. This absence left common people struggling to meet their basic needs and to feed the army.

In 1917, people in St. Petersburg protested the food shortages that arose as a result of the fighting.

Revolution

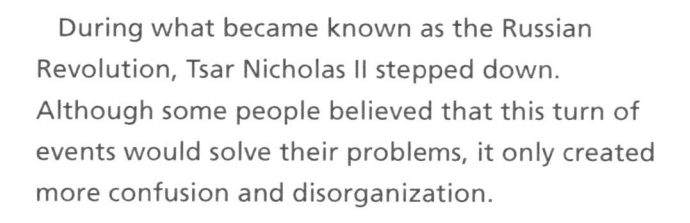

During what became known as the Russian Revolution, Tsar Nicholas II stepped down. Although some people believed that this turn of events would solve their problems, it only created more confusion and disorganization.

The Communists soon took over, under their chieftain Vladimir Lenin, and in 1918 announced the "Red Terror." Anyone who resisted, or didn't agree with them, or simply belonged to the wrong "class," was killed. This included the Tsar and his family, as well as officers in the old Russian Army (like Sanya's father, Isaaki), or just ordinary citizens. To protect themselves and Isaaki's memory, Sanya and his mother had to bury his father's war medals.

The "White" army formed to try and stop the "Red" Communists, and a Civil War ensued, as the two sides fought for control of the country. Millions died from war and hunger.

Tsar Nicholas II

The Communists' Red Army finally won this civil war in 1922 and announced that the country would no longer be called Russia. Instead they proclaimed a new nation called the Union of Soviet Socialist Republics (USSR), or the Soviet Union.

USSR

[yoo-es-es-**ar**]: **U**nion of **S**oviet **S**ocialist **R**epublics. The giant state that was formed after the Russian Revolution and the overthrow of the Tsars. At its zenith, it occupied one-sixth of the world's landmass, and was said to represent the coming triumph of Communism worldwide.

While people's freedoms were restricted under the Tsars, they were allowed to worship freely, to engage in free trade and own property. But such basic rights, as well as free speech and political debate, were no longer allowed under Communism. People were forced to do what the government said, or risk imprisonment and death.

Vladimir Lenin

The country was at war for the first three years of Sanya's life. When it ended, the new Communist government made things very difficult for Sanya and his family, and countless others. According to the Communist slogan—*from each according to his ability, to each according to his need*—all private property, such as Sanya's grandfather's farm, was now taken over by the government. His grandfather became homeless, then later was taken to the headquarters of the secret police and never seen again.

> **COMMUNISM**
>
> [**com**-yoo-ni-zum]: A system of government in which no resources, land, factories, farms or businesses were allowed to be owned privately. In the Soviet Union, these became the property of the government.

Sanya with his maternal grandfather (seated at left)

My grandfather was a very remarkable man. Actually, he replaced my father, because my father died before I was born. He began as a farm worker. Worked for several years, but so well that his employer ended up giving him a few sheep, a cow. I believe that was all. He started his farm just from that and raised it to such a high. Land was cheap there, so he started to buy. He created an estate of 5,400 acres, and was an important producer of corn and wool. When the revolution came, naturally he was dispossessed of all, had nothing to live on. So his farm workers supported him. As long as he remained free, they supported him. Everyone would load a cartload of goods for him. That was the kind of employer he was.[2]

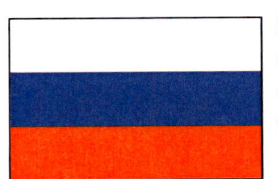

Russia flag: Represented Russia from 1883 until the Revolution in 1917. The design is over 300 years old and was first used by Peter the Great. When the Soviet Union expired in 1991, this original tricolored flag was restored.

USSR Flag: Represented the Soviet state from 1923 to 1991. The hammer stood for industry (workers), and the sickle for agriculture (peasants). The red star represented the Communist party.

Sanya's house in Rostov

Sanya grew up in Rostov, a southern port city, where his mother worked as a secretary. They lived in a small house, which had once been a horse stable. There was no running water or bathroom, and in the winter it was cold and drafty.

Sanya's mother

12

From an early age, Sanya wanted to be a writer. He wrote during the long hours while his mother worked. At ten, he started a magazine called *Twentieth Century*. The author of all the articles, he thought up names for writers of the various sections—news, events and science fiction. He even included games and puzzles, and kept records of how many imaginary people were reading his magazine.

in 7th grade, 1933

At fourteen, Sanya submitted some of his writing for publication. These early attempts were rejected. When he became an established author, he would look back on his early stories and describe them as "much of the usual youthful nonsense."

in university, 1938

13

As a teenager, Sanya took care of his mother, who was often sick with tuberculosis. He wanted to go to university in Moscow to study literature, but instead he stayed at home to help her. He studied math and physics because there was no writing program at Rostov University. Sanya was very good in these subjects but his first love was writing, which he continued whenever he could.

Like most people, Sanya wanted to fit in. In spite of what had been done to his grandfather, he believed in the Russian Revolution—as did most of his peers. He thought that the Revolution was the most earth-shaking event of modern world history. Sanya imagined it as a crazy whirlwind—a giant *Red Wheel*, spinning out of control and demolishing everything in its path.

> **RÉGIME**
> [ray-**zheem**]: A prevailing system of government, especially a repressive one.

His great wish was to write a book celebrating that revolution; little did he know that the régime it spawned would soon condemn him to prison.

2 *Dialogues with Solzhenitsyn.* Dir. Aleksandr Sokurov. Nadezhda Films, 1998.

Life Under Stalin

Throughout Sanya's teenage years, millions of people met the same tragic fate as his grandfather. Without cause they could lose their homes, be sent to prison or put to death. Six farmers were once executed for picking up clippings of hay after they had finished the harvest at their collective farm.

Joseph Stalin

COLLECTIVE FARM

A collective farm is one where the equipment, land and crops all belong to the government. Millions of farmers had their land taken away from them in the 1920s and 30s, and were forced instead to work these massive new government farms.

By the 1930s Joseph Stalin had come to power, and he ruled with an iron fist.

The USSR became a "telling society." People were encouraged to report family, friends, or anyone who said anything against the Communist government or Stalin.

Those reported were arrested and could be sentenced to the labor camps. Many were unjustly charged and sent away because a jealous friend or co-worker made an anonymous false accusation.

The prisoners in the camps were used as a source of free labor to construct buildings, canals and other projects for the USSR. People were often falsely accused because a project required certain kinds of experts. For example, if a building required the skills of an engineer, a man in that profession would be imprisoned. Families of these prisoners suffered too—they were held responsible for the same "crimes." Children were sent to labor camps, and those as young as twelve could be killed.

Stalin felt threatened by anyone who didn't agree with him, or could challenge his power.

2
ARRESTED

In 1941 Sanya, who was now twenty-two years old and went by his full name Aleksandr, graduated from university and, within months, enlisted in the Red Army to fight in World War II. Aleksandr's mathematical skills earned him a dangerous assignment in an artillery unit. He was awarded medals three times for bravery in battle and was promoted to First Lieutenant and then to Captain.

at the front, 1943

Marching over a thousand miles with his unit from 1942 to 1945, Aleksandr learned much about the horrors of war. He also came to know and revile Stalin's cruel treatment of Soviet citizens, who lived in fear and poverty.

Throughout the war, he exchanged letters with a university friend who was fighting in another unit. Aleksandr wrote about his concerns with Stalin and what changes should happen in their country after the war ended. He knew that the military police checked all mail for "thought crimes," so he referred to Stalin in code, calling him "the Guy with the Mustache" and

with university friend Vitkevich

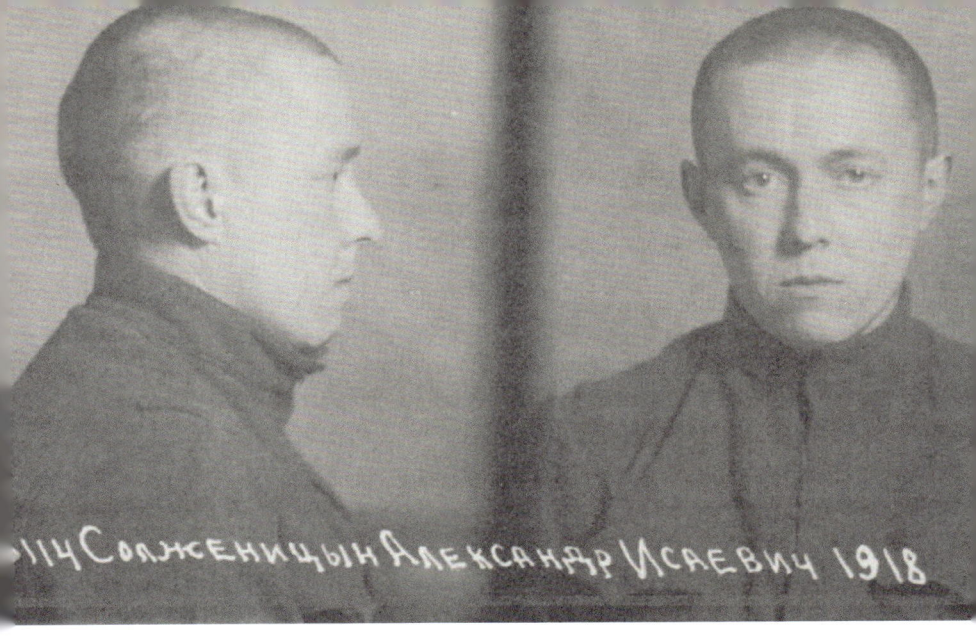

arrested

Pakhan [pa-**hahn**], or Boss. But this simple code proved no match for the police. Shortly before the end of the war, they arrested both Aleksandr, who was fighting on the front lines in Germany, and his university friend. All of Aleksandr's writing was confiscated.

Aleksandr was quite certain what the outcome would be before his secret trial occurred. He was marched to and from interrogation, day after day, while hearing victory salutes outside the prison for a war he was not allowed to finish fighting. The authorities accused him of being an enemy of Stalin and the government, and sentenced him to eight years of hard labor in the Gulag and *perpetual* (never-ending) exile after that.

> I'll never forget how I was brought into interrogation. In the middle of the room there was a huge pile of manuscripts. Somebody's apartment had been searched at night. And there lay that heap, and the investigator about to deal with it. An enormous heap, high in the form of a cone. A lot of manuscripts and books. The investigator was sitting at his table, far across from me. There was this mountain between us. And I thought, 'Now all is doomed.' Indeed, my war diaries were burned. Five notebooks all in all. I was deprived of these memories. All my notes from the front are gone.[3]

So Aleksandr worked as a bricklayer and laborer in various prison camps, where he dug clay and laid bricks in the heat of summer and in freezing-cold winter. Living conditions were bleak, as there was never sufficient food or clothing. Things could worsen at any time because of the way the camps were organized. Prisoners were forced to wear numbers, which were used instead of their names. If a member of a prisoner team said something wrong, didn't work hard enough, or got in trouble with the guards, everyone was punished, often by taking away food from the whole team.

at Kaluga Gate camp, 1946

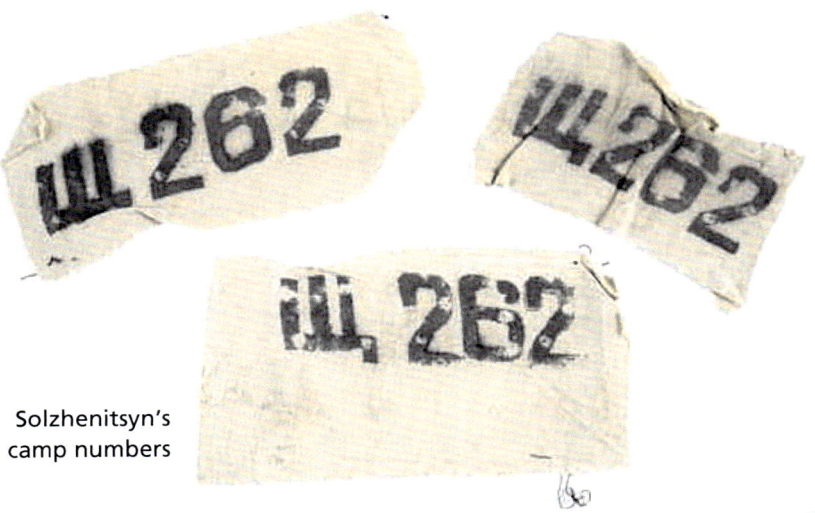

Solzhenitsyn's camp numbers

21

This method kept the prisoners from revolting.

> There is no worse moment than when you turn out for work parade in the morning. In the dark, in the freezing cold, with a hungry belly, and the whole day ahead of you.[4]

Fights among the prisoners were frequent. Not only did they mistrust the guards, they were fearful of one another. Men might gang up on a fellow prisoner responsible for group punishment. Their beatings could be as cruel as those inflicted by the guards, and sometimes ended in murder.

Aleksandr's earlier studies saved him from spending his entire prison term in the harsh conditions of the labor camps. He spent four years—about half of it—in various *sharashkas* [sha-**rosh**-kas] (secret research-and-development laboratories). In between working on technical projects, Aleksandr took advantage of the easier physical conditions by offering and taking informal classes in art, science and history.

the Marfino *sharashka* (the setting of *In the First Circle*)

Aleksandr continued to write, but knew he had to keep it a secret. He often committed a story to memory until he was lucky enough to find a small piece of paper on which to write it down.

> In the interval between two barrowloads of mortar I would put my bit of paper on the bricks and (without letting my neighbors see what I was doing) write down with a pencil stub the verses which had rushed into my head while I was slapping on the last hodful.[5]

prayer rosary used by Aleksandr to keep track of thousands of lines of memorized poetry

Over his prison years, he wrote a 9,000-line poem that he repeated over and over again until he was finally able to write it down after he had served his sentence. Destroying any scrap of paper after first memorizing it was the only way to make sure the guards would not discover his writing.

EXILE

[**eck**-zyle]: Being forced to leave one's home and denied the ability to return. In Russia, and later in the USSR, one was sent to faraway places, such as Siberia, the vast, sparsely populated northeastern part of the country. The Soviet form of exile also carried very severe restrictions. The prisoner could not stray more than thirty miles from the town without special permission.

Aleksandr's experience as a prisoner changed him. He became thoroughly opposed to Communism and the Revolution. Once he learned the truth of what was happening in the Gulag, he wanted to let the Russian people know.

> I hate to think what sort of writer I would have become (for I would have gone on writing) if I had not been *put inside*.[6]

Aleksandr finished his eight-year sentence but, instead of being freed, found himself exiled for life to Kok-Terek, Kazakhstan in the southern USSR.

in Kok-Terek hut, on the edge of the desert

with his math students in Kok-Terek

Unlike in the labor camps, here he was able to walk around freely and even to teach school. Still, his freedom was limited, as he was forbidden to travel more than thirty miles from the town, and it was impossible to receive visits from friends or family. Although he was allowed to use pen and paper, he still had to write his thoughts and ideas in secret.

In addition to the harsh conditions of the Gulag, Aleksandr had an additional trial to endure—cancer. He had been operated on for cancer while in the labor camps, only to have the disease return forcefully in exile.

> In autumn 1953 it looked very much as though I had only a few months to live. In December the doctors—comrades in exile—confirmed that I had at most three weeks left.
>
> All that I had memorized in the camps ran the risk of extinction together with the head that held it.
>
> This was a dreadful moment in my life: to die on the threshold of freedom, to see all I had written, all that gave meaning to my life thus far, about to perish with me.[7]

Aleksandr was afraid that his honest truths about Communism and the camps would never be read. Before he left for the cancer clinic, he put his writings inside bottles and buried them in a garden. Would they be found? If they were found, would they be read? If the Communists uncovered them, would he be shot?

---

3 *Dialogues with Solzhenitsyn*. Dir. Aleksandr Sokurov, Nadezhda Films, 1998.
4 *One Day in the Life of Ivan Denisovich*, trans. H. T. Willetts, New York: Farrar, Straus and Giroux, 2014, p. 28.
5 *The Gulag Archipelago*, trans. Harry Willetts, New York: Harper Perennial Modern Classics, 2007, vol. 3, part V, chapter 5, p. 104.
6 *The Oak and the Calf*, trans. H. T. Willetts, New York: Harper & Row, 1981, p. 2.
7 *The Oak and the Calf*, trans. H. T. Willetts, New York: Harper & Row, 1981, p. 3

3

AMNESTY

[**am**-nes-tee]: A pardon given by the government, especially for political prisoners.

FREEDOM TO TELL THE TRUTH

In 1953 Stalin died and Nikita Khrushchev became the new leader of the Soviet Union. Three years later, in 1956, those jailed for opposing Stalin were given amnesty. It meant that Aleksandr, having beaten back cancer, was also free to return home to Russia.

writing in Ryazan

teaching in Ryazan

Aleksandr settled in Ryazan, a medium-sized city not far from Moscow, and again taught math in school. He continued to write but was very careful:

> I had never once gone to bed without making sure that everything was hidden, and rehearsing my behavior in case there was a knock in the night.[8]

To further protect his work, he would hide chapters of his books with different friends.

As an "underground" writer, he had a number of problems to deal with.

> Where and how the work is to be kept, under what cover it will be transported, what new hiding places must be devised as the volume of writings and of copies steadily grows.[9]

It is frustrating to write and not be able to have your word read by others. Aleksandr wanted people to know about the Soviet labor camps and their cruel conditions. He wanted the whole world to know the truth, so that the lives of those killed might be remembered. Could he now tell the story of what had happened to so many Russians in the camps without putting in peril his own life and the lives of those he loved and cared about?

THAW

From 1962 to 1964, the politics of the USSR were slightly relaxed. It was during this period that Aleksandr was able to publish *One Day in the Life of Ivan Denisovich*.

Aleksandr decided to take a chance. With the help of friends and with the eventual approval of Khrushchev, the head of the Soviet Union, his book *One Day in the Life of Ivan Denisovich* was published in 1962 in a magazine called *Novyi Mir* [**no**-vee-**meer**], which means "new world." This book told the story of one prisoner's day in a labor camp.

Moscow, in front of the *Novyi Mir* building

> On one long winter workday in camp, as I was lugging a handbarrow together with another man, I asked myself how one might portray the totality of our camp existence. In essence it should suffice

31

to give a thorough description of a single day, providing minute details and focusing on the most ordinary kind of worker; that would reflect the entirety of our experience. It wouldn't even be necessary to give examples of any particular horrors. It shouldn't be an extraordinary day at all, but rather a completely unremarkable one, the kind of day that will add up to years. That was my conception, and it lay dormant in my mind for nine years. [10]

special *Novyi Mir* cover for *Ivan Denisovich*

Millions of copies of *Ivan Denisovich* were circulated from hand to hand in the Soviet Union. It was translated into different languages so that people all over the world could read it. Those outside of the USSR hailed the author as a "truth-teller," while the ordinary Soviet citizen now had confirmation of the stories of family and friends who had been in the camps.

in November 1962

The New York Times wrote,

This quiet tale has struck a powerful blow against the return of the horrors of the Stalin system. For Solzhenitsyn's words burn like acid.[11]

Major Leaders of Russia and the Soviet Union
SINCE 1894

1894-1917: Emperor Nicholas the Second (the last tsar). Abdicated in 1917, executed in 1918.

1917-1924: Vladimir Lenin (the first Soviet leader). Ruled until his death.

1924-1953: Joseph Stalin. Ruled until his death.

1955-1964: Nikita Khrushchev. Deposed by Brezhnev.

1964-1982: Leonid Brezhnev. Ruled until his death.

1985-1991: Mikhail Gorbachov (the last Soviet leader). Resigned.

1991-1999: Boris Yeltsin (the first President of Russia). Resigned.

1999- Vladimir Putin.

Aleksandr continued to use his writing to tell about conditions in the USSR, not only the labor camps, but also present-day situations. He also wrote about his experience as a patient in *Cancer Ward*.

the cancer ward in Tashkent where Aleksandr was treated

About surviving cancer, Aleksandr wrote,

> All the life that has been given back to me has not been mine in the full sense: it is built around a purpose. [12]

35

Part of that purpose was to make sure that people understood the horrors of the Gulag. Now that he was well known, many people who had been in the prisons wanted to tell him their stories. While *One Day in the Life of Ivan Denisovich* related the life of one prisoner in the Gulag, *The Gulag Archipelago* was based on the stories of over two hundred camp survivors. It also included a history of the prison system dating back to 1918. At the beginning of this book Aleksandr wrote,

> I dedicate this to all those who did not live to tell it. And may they please forgive me for not having seen it all nor remembered it all.[13]

The "thaw," or relaxing of the government rule in the Soviet Union under Khrushchev, didn't last long. By

1964 Khrushchev had been forced out of office, and the new leaders again tightened censorship. Aleksandr would secretly pass his manuscripts to people who dared to read them even while knowing they could be punished. Because the USSR did not allow copiers, some people spent nights retyping the banned books, producing *samizdat* for other free thinkers to read. Some of the illegal copies were smuggled to the West, translated and published.

> **CENSORSHIP**
>
> [**sen**-sur-ship]: A government deciding what people can read, what movies they can see. A repressive government uses censorship as a way to control what people know.

> **MANUSCRIPT**
>
> [**man**-yoo-skript]: An author's writing, before it becomes printed as a book.

manuscript of *Cancer Ward*

One person who became "a soldier of the samizdat" was Natalia Svetlova, who wrote, "I was a very fast typist and spent a lot of time at the typewriter." She also helped in getting books to people who wanted to read them. It was through this activity that Aleksandr met Natalia, his future wife and helpmate.

Aleksandr's books were translated into many different languages so people all over the world could read them. This brought pressure on the Soviet Union to treat their citizens more humanely, but still it resisted doing so.

Natalia Svetlova

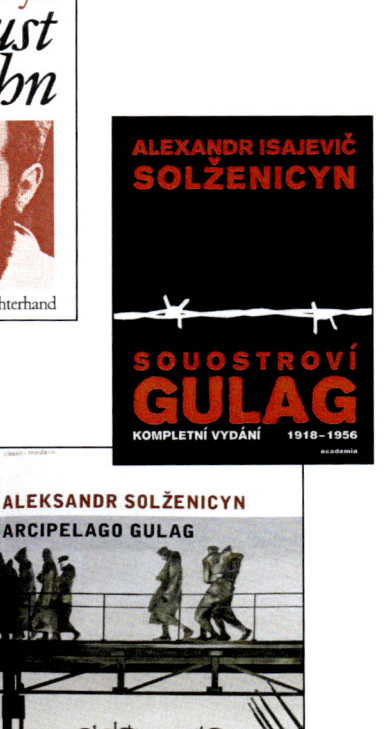

8 *The Oak and the Calf*, trans. H. T. Willetts, New York: Harper & Row, 1981, p. 13.
9 *The Oak and the Calf*, trans. H. T. Willetts, New York: Harper & Row, 1981, p. 5.
10 Interview with Barry Holland, BBC Radio Russian Service, 8 June 1982. Quoted in Daniel J. Mahoney, *The Other Solzhenitsyn*, St. Augustine's Press 2014, pp. 209-10.
11 Harrison E. Salisbury, *New York Times Book Review*, 22 January 1963.
12 *The Oak and the Calf*, trans. H. T. Willetts, New York: Harper & Row, 1981, p. 4.
13 *The Gulag Archipelago*, trans. Thomas P. Whitney, New York: Harper Perennial Modern Classics, 2007, vol. 1, dedication.

LIFE magazine,
23 June 1972

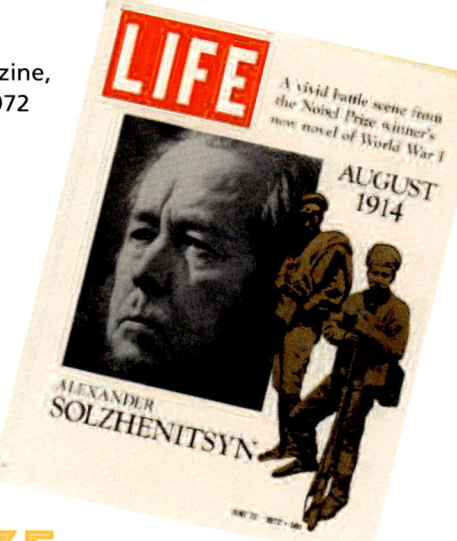

4

NOBEL-PRIZE WINNER

While people in the USSR had to read Aleksandr's books in secret, they were read openly elsewhere in the world, and he was acknowledged as a hugely talented writer.

NOBEL PRIZE

[no-**bel**]: International prizes awarded each year to those who "have conferred the greatest benefit on mankind" through their outstanding achievement in the fields of physics, chemistry, medicine, literature, economics, and the promotion of peace. The award was established in 1895 by Alfred Nobel, the inventor of dynamite.

40

In 1970 he was awarded the Nobel Prize for Literature, the highest award an author can receive. First bestowed in 1901, Nobel prizes are awarded in six areas for those who confer the "greatest benefit on mankind." Anyone in the world is eligible to win.

Explaining their choice of Aleksandr for the Prize, the Swedish Academy said of his writings,

> . . . they speak to us of matters that we need to hear more than ever before.[14]

The Academy also noted that he was chosen

> for the ethical force with which he has pursued the indispensable traditions of Russian literature.[15]

The Nobel Academy recognized both the power of his writing and its ability to make the world aware of the inhumane conditions in the USSR. Aleksandr was now part of the great tradition of Russian writers, whose work included plays, novels and poetry. In addition to Aleksandr, four other Russians have been awarded the honor of the Nobel Prize for Literature.

Ivan Bunin, 1933 laureate

Boris Pasternak, 1958 laureate

Mikhail Sholokhov, 1965 laureate

Joseph Brodsky, 1987 laureate

As much as he would have liked to go and receive this award in Stockholm, he was afraid to leave the Soviet Union: the government hinted that if he left the country, with or without his wife (who was then pregnant with his first child), he would not be allowed to return. Aleksandr had lived in exile before, and never wanted to do it again. He also wanted his child to be born in the land of his own birth.

with sons Yermolai and Ignat

It was not until 1974 that Aleksandr and his wife traveled to Stockholm to accept this award. Like so many recipients before him, he wrote a Nobel-Prize lecture.

accepting the Nobel from the Swedish king, December 1974

To have mounted this rostrum from which the Nobel lecture is delivered— a platform placed at the disposal of but few writers and then only once in a lifetime—I have climbed not the three or four attached steps, but hundreds and even thousands of them, with almost no toehold, steep, and covered with ice, leading out of the darkness and cold where it had been my fate to survive while others—perhaps more gifted and stronger than I—perished.

the front and back of Solzhenitsyn's medal

45

> ... And today, accompanied by the shades of the fallen, as with bowed head I permit others who were worthy earlier to precede me to this platform—how am I today to surmise and to express what they would have wished to say?
>
> ... The favorite proverbs in Russian are about *truth*. They forcefully express a long and difficult national experience, sometimes in striking fashion:
>
> *One word of truth shall outweigh the whole world.*[16]

Aleksandr believed strongly in the survival of good in an evil world, and in the power of the spoken word, through art and in books, to ultimately change things for the better. The world would soon find out how right he was.

---

14 Nobelprize.org. Nobel Media AB 2014 nobelprize.org/nobel_prizes/literature/laureates/1970/press.html. Accessed on 4 December 2014.
15 "The Nobel Prize in Literature 1970". Nobelprize.org. Nobel Media AB 2014. nobelprize.org/nobel_prizes/literature/laureates/1970/ Accessed on 4 December 2014.
16 *Nobel Lecture*, trans. Alexis Klimoff, published in The Solzhenitsyn Reader: New and Essential Writings 1947-2005, ed. Edward E. Ericson, Jr. and Daniel J. Mahoney, Wilmington: ISI Books, 2006, pp. 515 and 526.

5

EXILED AGAIN

People all around the world admired Aleksandr's writing, but the Soviet government, of course, did not, since they viewed Aleksandr as a threat to their system. When he won the Nobel Prize, the chief of the KGB (the secret police) wrote in a memo,

> If Solzhenitsyn continues to reside in the country after receiving the Nobel Prize, it will strengthen his position, and allow him to propagate his views more actively. [17]

One day in 1971, while Aleksandr was standing in line at a department store, KGB agents sidled up next to him and managed to rub a poison on his skin without his being aware of it. Based on his symptoms, and the later account of an officer involved in that operation,

RICIN

[**rye-**sin]: a highly toxic poison, lethal even in tiny doses.

it is now thought that the poison was ricin, which is highly toxic and often results in death.

I certainly did not feel it, but by mid-morning the skin on my left side suddenly started to hurt a great deal […] I had a very large burn. The following morning I was reduced to a terrible state: my left hip, left side, stomach and back were covered with blisters.[18]

co-ordinated press attack

It took Aleksandr months to recover from this attack but it did not keep him from writing. It was becoming clear that the Communists wanted him silenced, so they hounded him in the press and the KGB continued to threaten him and his family. He knew he could be arrested at any moment, so he and his wife Natalia made sure his books were hidden in safe places.

the dreaded KGB headquarters on Lubyanka Square in Moscow

Stig Fredriskon, a reporter for Swedish Television (SVT), was among several brave journalists and diplomats who helped to smuggle Aleksandr's writings out of the Soviet Union. Since Stig and Aleksandr both were fathers of young children, they pushed their baby carriages in the park or on the street and, when they stopped to admire each other's baby, would pass manuscripts.

Stig Fredriskon

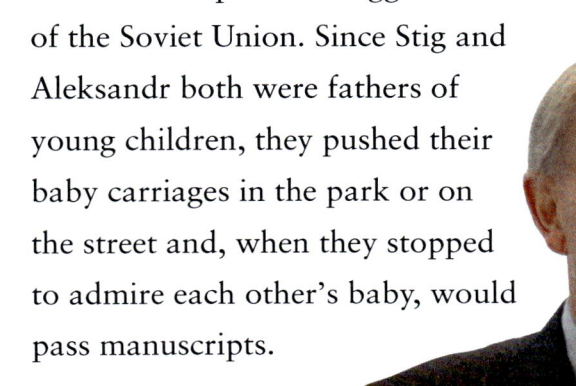

The story of my secret meetings with Solzhenitsyn has ingredients of a spy thriller. We had to act like secret agents. But in contrast to the novels, everything was true. Nothing was ever written down between us, all the arrangements about time and place for the meetings were kept in our heads. We had alternate dates, and reserve dates for the alternates, if something made it impossible for one of us to show up. I had also thought of the possibility that he might need an urgent meeting with me; normally there were a few weeks between our meetings. I proposed that he call me on my telephone in the office early in the morning before my Soviet secretary arrived at nine. But wasn't the telephone tapped? Yes, but I told Solzhenitsyn to pretend to make a wrong call. Call my number and ask: "Hello, is this the dry-cleaner's?" or "Is this the home delivery service of the Gastronom?" People made wrong calls in Moscow all the time, it happened almost daily, and when it happened you just said "you've got the wrong number" and slammed the receiver down. If Solzhenitsyn made a wrong call to me, the KGB might not react. But I would immediately recognize his voice, even if he only asked for the dry-cleaner's, and it would be the signal. It meant that something has happened and we had to meet at once.[19]

Since they were unsuccessful in quietly killing him, the KGB decided to expel Aleksandr from the Soviet Union after *The Gulag Archipelago* was published in France in late 1973. They forced their way into his apartment, pushed him against the wall and said, "you will come with us."

first edition of *Gulag*, Paris (1973)

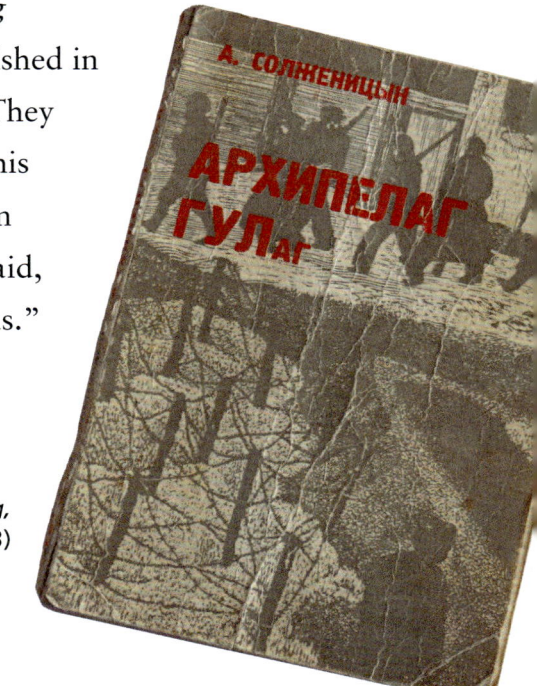

Why the Soviet Union Was Afraid of Aleksandr

The most powerful weapon against evil is truth telling. By writing the truth, Aleksandr brought attention to the horrors of Soviet reality. He based his novels on the everyday life of people in prisons, labor camps, hospitals, schools, collective farms—all people he met. And once his works were published, hundreds of people secretly reached out to him to tell him their experience in the camps. He collected their stories into a blistering documentary about the Soviet system of injustice—the famed *Gulag Archipelago*—which finally turned the world against the Soviets.

slave labor at the White Sea Canal, 1932

Because there were papers that he didn't want the KGB to see, Aleksandr tried to leave as quickly as possible.

> The one thing I remembered to do was to dress prison-fashion, shabbily [...] I put on an old cap and a sheepskin coat which I had worn in exile [...] I said no goodbyes [...] except to my wife [...] We kissed each other goodbye, unhurriedly, and with the realization returning that it might be forever [...] I made the sign of the cross slowly over my wife. And she blessed me [...] 'Look after the children.'[20]

Without looking back, Aleksandr left with the KGB agents.

KGB

[kay-gee-**bee**]: **K**omitet **G**osudarstvennoi **B**ezopasnosti—the Committee for Government Security—the Soviet Union's dreaded secret police.

entrance to the Solzhenitsyns' apartment building

In the apartment where Aleksandr lived, there were copies of many writings by him and others. Because these would be viewed as anti-Soviet, and could result in other people being arrested, his wife Natalia gathered up papers and started burning them as quickly as she could. It was a difficult task to keep a watchful eye on her young sons while destroying materials that could endanger others. At one point, because the KGB agents had broken the lock on the door, her 18-month-old son crawled out of the apartment and could have been seriously hurt if he had fallen down the stairs.

Aleksandr was taken to prison and charged with treason.

TREASON

[**tree**-zun]: The purposeful betrayal of one's country, usually to benefit another. Solzhenitsyn was falsely charged with treason in order to provide a plausible excuse for his expulsion.

He realized they could shoot him or keep him imprisoned for many years. However, he also figured that, because he was known throughout the world, it would not look good for the Soviets to pursue either course. And indeed, they decided to strip him of his citizenship and expel him.

He was put on a plane and sent to Germany.

EXPEL

[eck-**spell**]: To forcibly remove a person from a place or a whole country.

the fateful edict of the Supreme Soviet

the Aeroflot plane used to deport Solzhenitsyn

Aleksandr compared this to his World-War-II experience, when he left Russia to fight in Germany and was then arrested and returned to Moscow.

> I am leaving Russia for the second time. The first time was with our advancing army, in a front-line truck [...] And just once, I had returned: from Germany, all the way to Moscow, with three Geebees [KGB] for companions. And now I was leaving Moscow with others of their kind, eight of them this time. It was like my arrest in reverse.[21]

When he landed, the reporters wanted him to make a statement. Instead he said,

> I said quite enough while I was in the Soviet Union. Now I shall be silent for a while.[22]

What did this mean? For such an outspoken writer this seemed a contradiction, but for Aleksandr the answer was simple. His life had been spared: the best use he could make of it was to use his time wisely and continue to write and publish his books.

press throng awaiting a statement from Solzhenitsyn

17 Secret memorandum of KGB chief Yuri Andropov, published in "Intelligence and Security Committee, The Mitrokhin Inquiry Report", Cm 4764, June 13, 2000, p. 4. Quoted in Christopher Andrew and Vasili Mitrokhin, *The Sword and the Shield: The Mitrokhin Archive and the Secret History of the KGB*, Basic Books, 2000.
18 *Washington Post*, 21 April 1992.
19 Stig Fredrikson, "How I Helped Alexandr Solzhenitsyn Smuggle His Nobel Lecture from the USSR". Nobelprize.org. Nobel Media AB 2014. nobelprize.org/nobel_prizes/literature/laureates/1970/solzhenitsyn-article.html Accessed on 4 December 2014.
20 *The Oak and the Calf*, trans. H. T. Willetts, New York: Harper & Row, 1981, pp. 410-11.
21 *The Oak and the Calf*, trans. H. T. Willetts, New York: Harper & Row, 1981, p. 443.
22 *The Oak and the Calf*, trans. H. T. Willetts, New York: Harper & Row, 1981, p. 451

6

IN THE WEST

Within three weeks of finding himself exiled to the West, Aleksandr had decided to settle in Zurich, Switzerland, while waiting for his wife, children and mother-in-law to join him. It took another few weeks before Aleksandr could race up the airplane steps and embrace his sons at last.

29 March 1974

Natalia had refused to leave Russia sooner, saying that one, then another, of the boys was sick with pneumonia. But the real reason was that she was busy smuggling out, piece by little piece, several suitcases' worth of priceless papers—drafts of Aleksandr's unpublished writings, research materials about the Revolution, eyewitness accounts of major events.

> **THE WEST**
>
> The free countries of Western Europe, North America, and Asia Pacific, largely united by shared cultural values, political ideas ("free peoples, free markets") and a common Communist threat.

Each item had to be hidden under a winter coat and carried out in full view of the KGB, who were watching the family's apartment around the clock. Were it not for brave friends—many of them Western journalists and diplomats—the main work of Aleksandr's life, *The Red Wheel*, would have remained unfinished forever. So grateful was Aleksandr that, despite being pressed from every side by urgent tasks, he set them aside and sat down instead to write *The Invisible Allies*, a tribute to those who risked so much to help Aleksandr and his call for a free Russia. That book was eventually published in the early 1990s, when the identities of his allies could at last be revealed safely.

> **ARCHIVE**
>
> [**ar**-kive]: A collection of materials—books, newspapers, public documents, private letters, and other "primary sources"— used by a researcher to understand the essence of his object of study.

Meanwhile, life in Zurich, at the crossroads of Europe, proved hugely stressful for Aleksandr and his family. Dozens of visitors every day would stop by their modest Zurich home, hoping to meet the famous writer, and KGB agents continued to track Aleksandr closely. Consequently, the family began to search for a place to live where Aleksandr would have the peace and quiet he needed to write.

the Solzhenitsyns in Zurich

in Washington, D.C., 1975

In the meantime, the United States Senate had introduced a resolution to make Aleksandr an honorary citizen of the U.S.A., and his travels there had left a strong positive impression on him. Furthermore, the best archives for his research on Russian history were chiefly located in American universities.

at Stanford University, 1975

Admired and welcomed by many in America, Aleksandr and his family decided to leave Switzerland and move to Cavendish, Vermont in 1976.

Cavendish, Vermont

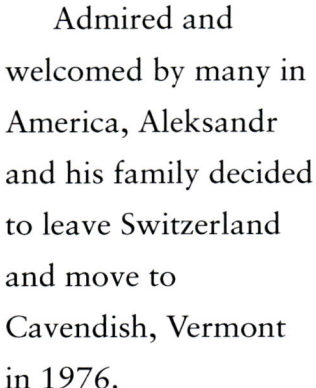

Aleksandr talked to his new neighbors at Town Meeting about how this was the first home he ever had.

In all my life I have never had any definite permanent place to live, much less my own home.

1977 Town Meeting

> **TOWN MEETING**
>
> A meeting open to voters of a town, who, together, make decisions about how the town is to be run. This is a common form of local government in Vermont and other New England states.

Not knowing the conditions of Soviet life, you can barely imagine that people in the Soviet Union are not allowed to live where they choose [...] Finally, the Soviet authorities would no longer tolerate me at all, and deported me from the USSR [...] It so happened that among you, in Cavendish, Vermont, I was able to find my first home and my first permanent residence. I am no fan of big cities with their bustling way of life; but I like very much your simple way of life [...] I like the landscape that surrounds you, and I like very much your climate, with its long snowy winters which remind me of Russia.[23]

Aleksandr asked the people of Cavendish to respect his need for privacy. He was not only concerned that the Soviets would find and harm him or his family, but he also wanted a quiet place where he could write and not be interrupted.

Aleksandr also wanted his neighbors to know that there was a difference between Russians and Soviets. "Soviet" was the type of Communist government that the Russian people had to live under.

> 'Russian' is to 'Soviet' as 'man' is to 'disease.' We do not call someone afflicted with cancer—'Cancer,' or someone with the plague—'Plague,' for we understand that their disease, their severe trial, is not their fault.[24]

Aleksandr ended his talk by saying,

> The Communist system is a disease, a plague that has been spreading across the earth for many years already, and it is impossible to predict what peoples will yet be forced to experience this disease firsthand. My people, the Russians, have been suffering from it for sixty years already; they long to be healed. And the day will come when they are indeed healed of this Soviet disease. On that day I will thank you for being good friends and neighbors, and will go back to my homeland.[25]

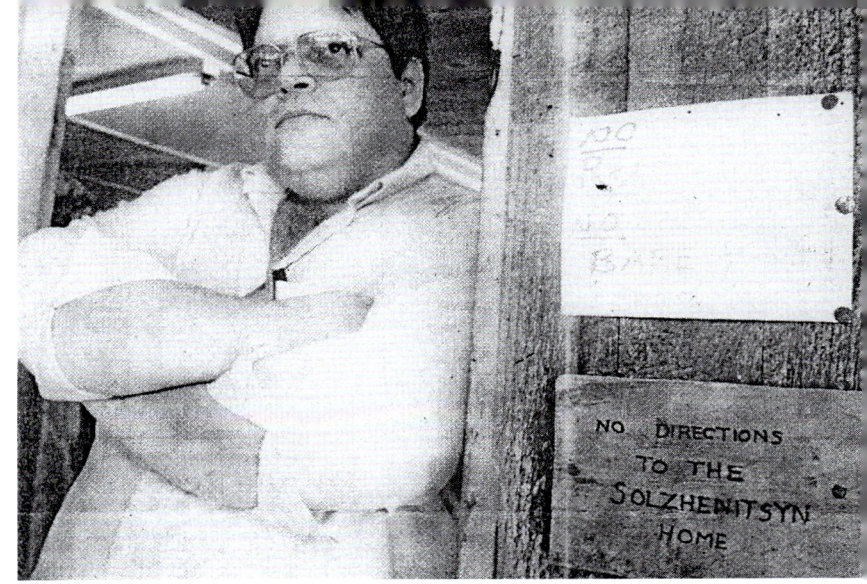

General Store sign

The people of Cavendish left Aleksandr alone and protected him from outsiders who wanted to bother him. The owner of the local store hung a sign that said, "No service for shirtless or shoeless customers and No directions to the Solzhenitsyn home."

For many years, Aleksandr had been acutely aware that the tumultuous events and circumstances of his life—the war, prison, camp, cancer, and his titanic battle with the Soviet government—had continually interfered with his main goal of writing *The Red Wheel*, the real story of the Russian Revolution. He was first seized by the dream of writing such a book on a November day in 1936, at seventeen years old, and immediately began to research and write. But other books always seemed more *urgent*, and years passed. Yet Aleksandr's sense of unshakable mission persevered as stubbornly as those early manuscripts themselves, while his understanding and knowledge of the Revolution deepened and evolved. At long last it was here in Cavendish, far removed in space and time from the revolutionary streets of 1917 Petrograd, that Aleksandr was able to find the time, the quiet and the resources to plunge himself into history and to fulfill

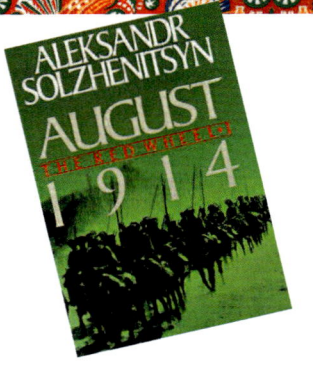

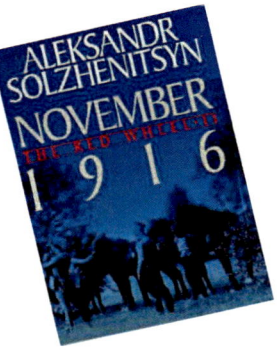

editing with Natalia

Cavendish, 1982

the mission he had cherished since youth. After years of research and writing, Aleksandr finally completed *The Red Wheel* in 1989, fifty-three years after first conceiving it.

Natalia worked just as hard as her husband. She not only read, edited, researched and dealt with his publishers, but also raised their three boys and managed the Solzhenitsyn Foundation: Aleksandr had used all the money from sales of *The Gulag Archipelago* to set up this fund to help camp prisoners and their families. Like the secret printing and reading of Aleksandr's books, this fund's work had to be carried out undercover throughout the 1970s and 80s. Natalia would later recall that

> Our life was so intensive because of our work— it felt like the office of a major literary magazine. If we had ended up in a large city, that would have slowed down our pace considerably. We couldn't have kept up the crazy pace we set for ourselves in Vermont.[26]

Yermolai helps to typeset, 1983

The Fall of Communism and the Soviet Union

There were many factors that led to the downfall of the Soviet Union. More than half of the people in the Soviet Union did not identify themselves as Russian, and many did not want to be part of the USSR. Russians themselves were tired of Communist oppression and the burden of ruling over others. Communism did not provide the lifestyle that most people wanted. In August 1991 demonstrations and protests took place all over the USSR. The military refused to fight, saying they could not fire on their fellow countrymen. Without the military it would be almost impossible for the Communists to remain in power. By December 1991 the Soviet Union no longer existed. It had broken up into Russia and fourteen newly independent countries.

math lesson, 1978

While Aleksandr wrote every day, he also spent time with his children, teaching them Russian, history, math and physics. As he would later say of those years,

I wrote and I waited.

at self-made desk in the woods

After eighteen years, the wait was over. Russia became a country again, and the Soviet government was no more. While Aleksandr's citizenship was restored in 1990, he remained in Cavendish to finish *The Red Wheel* and related writings before returning to Russia in 1994.

Before he left, Aleksandr spoke to his neighbors one last time at Town Meeting.

1994 Town Meeting

> I have worked here for almost eighteen years. It has been the most productive period in my life. I have done all that I wanted to do.

[...] Our children grew up and went to school here, alongside your children. For them, Vermont is home. Indeed, our whole family has felt at home among you. Exile is always difficult, and yet I could not imagine a better place to live, and wait, and wait for my return home than Cavendish, Vermont.[27]

---

23 Speech at Cavendish Town Meeting, 28 February 1977.
24 Speech at Cavendish Town Meeting, 28 February 1977.
25 Speech at Cavendish Town Meeting, 28 February 1977.
26 Jay Nordlinger, "Wife and Soldier", National Review Online, 10 January 2013. Accessed on 4 December 2014.
27 Speech at Cavendish Town Meeting, 28 February 1994, published in *The Solzhenitsyn Reader: New and Essential Writings* 1947-2005, ed. Edward E. Ericson, Jr. and Daniel J. Mahoney, Wilmington: ISI Books, 2006, p. 607.

7

HOME AT LAST

Aleksandr was thrilled to return home, and spent much of his first year traveling extensively around the country. He was saddened to see how people were living. People did not know how to adjust to this new life. Many did not have jobs, and a number of the social programs, including pensions and health care, were not available in the manner they once were.

Yaroslavl Station, Moscow, July 21, 1994

73

Magadan, May 27, 1994

Vladivostok, May 27, 1994

The old Communist system had been dismantled and discredited, yet little thought had been given to the human cost of building a new society from scratch. Change was happening, but Aleksandr, like most Russians, believed it was too fast for ordinary people to bear. Still, Aleksandr believed in them and in Russia.

Ovsianka, 1994

Vladivostok, May 27, 1994

an exchange of views

Having traveled far and wide across Russia these past four years, having watched, having listened, I am willing to state, under oath if need be: No, our Spirit yet lives! In its core it is uncorrupted! [...] Yes, the *Spirit* is capable of reversing the direction

Ryazan, 1994

Primorye, 1994

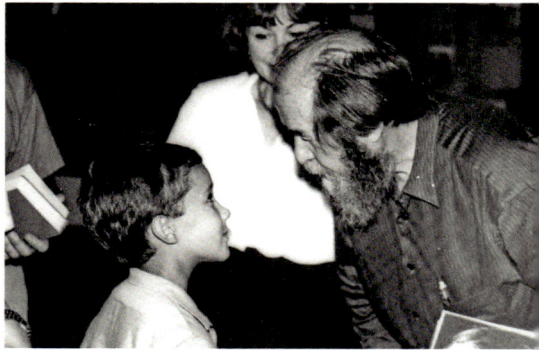

Omsk, 1994

of even the most fatal process. It can pull us back even from the brink [...] despite a crushing century for Russians, there is hope for us yet. It has not been taken away.[28]

Borovsk, 1994

> **GENRE**
>
> [**zhahn**-ruh]: Type of literary composition, e.g., novel, novella, short story, play, biography, poem.

Living in the woods on the outskirts of Moscow, Aleksandr made almost one hundred appearances during his first year back. However, declining health eventually limited his public activities in subsequent years. Still, he wrote every day, and resumed writing in certain genres—short stories and miniatures—that he'd abandoned while living in the West.

In 2007 Aleksandr was voted the State Award of the Russian Federation for "outstanding achievements in the field of humanities." The President of Russia went to Aleksandr's home to deliver the prize, and praised him for "dedicating his life to Russia."

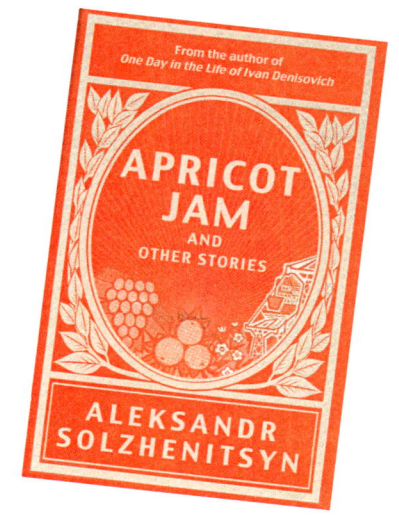

at home with family, Moscow, 2003

Aleksandr's grave

Aleksandr died at the age of 89, on August 3, 2008, and was buried at Donskoy Monastery in Moscow. In a condolence message to his family, the Russian President said,

Aleksandr Isayevich gave his entire life to his Fatherland, served his country as a true citizen and patriot and devoted himself

78

with all his heart to the fate of the Russian people and a fair and just system for the country's life [...] The passing of this great man, one of the greatest thinkers, writers and humanists of the twentieth century, is an irreplaceable loss for Russia and the entire world.[29]

From the time he was a child, Aleksandr knew that he was meant to be a writer. Through the hardships of war, camps, cancer, persecution, and exile from his beloved Russia, he saw and wrote about the worst and best of what people could do to one another. He used his own life and experiences to tell the story of his country. With the help and support of his wife, family and friends, he created a body of literature that changed the history of Russia and the world. His life was not always easy, but it was filled with purpose and meaning.

In 2009 his book *The Gulag Archipelago* was included on the required reading list for Russian high-school students. What an important healing step this was after the Soviet era when Aleksandr's books were completely banned.

Aleksandr's words and books continue to inspire people. Quotes from his writings are used frequently to explain difficult and inhumane situations all over the world. Aleksandr's words are timeless and powerful. As he reminded us, *one word of truth shall outweigh the whole world.*

Economist cover, August 9, 2008

> I am of course confident that I shall fulfill my duty as a writer in all circumstances—from the grave even more successfully and incontrovertibly than in my lifetime. No one can bar the road to truth, and to advance its cause I am prepared to accept even death. But may it be that repeated lessons will finally teach us not to stay the writer's pen during his lifetime?[30]

28 *Russia in Collapse*, trans. Stephan Solzhenitsyn, published in *The Solzhenitsyn Reader: New and Essential Writings 1947-2005*, ed. Edward E. Ericson, Jr. and Daniel J. Mahoney, Wilmington: ISI Books, 2006, p. 483.
29 President Dmitri Medvedev, telegram to Solzhenitsyn family, eng.kremlin.ru/news/19188 Accessed on 4 December 2014.
30 Letter to the Fourth Congress of the Union of Soviet Writers, 16 May 1967. Quoted in *The Oak and the Calf,* trans. H. T. Willetts, New York: Harper & Row, 1981, p. 462.

GLOSSARY

Amnesty [**am**-nes-tee]: A pardon given by the government, especially for political prisoners.

Archive [**ar**-kive]: A collection of materials—books, newspapers, public documents, private letters, and other "primary sources"—used by a researcher to understand the essence of his object of study.

Censorship [**sen**-sur-ship]: A government deciding what people can read, what movies they can see. A repressive government uses censorship as a way to control what people know.

Cold War: Intense political struggle between countries, but no outright war. "The Cold War" took place between the Soviet Union and the West starting at the end of World War II. It ended in 1990. While there was a race to see who could put a man on the moon first, and who had more weapons, and several bloody "proxy" wars, there was no direct military conflict.

Collective farm: A collective farm is one where the equipment, land and crops all belong to the government. Millions of farmers had their land taken away from them in the 1920s and 30s, and were forced instead to work these massive new government farms.

Communism [**com**-yoo-ni-zum]**:** A system of government in which no resources, land, factories, farms or businesses were allowed to be owned privately. In the Soviet Union, these became the property of the government.

Exile [**eck**-zyle]: Being forced to leave one's home and denied the ability to return. In Russia, and later in the USSR, one was sent to faraway places, such as Siberia, the vast, sparsely populated northeastern part of the country. The Soviet form of exile also carried very severe restrictions. The prisoner could not stray more than thirty miles from the town without special permission.

Expel [eck-**spell**]: To forcibly remove a person from a place or a whole country.

Genre [**zhahn**-ruh]: Type of literary composition, e.g., novel, novella, short story, play, biography, poem.

Gulag [**goo**-log]: The Russian abbreviation for Chief Administration of Corrective Labor Camps and Colonies. This was the Soviet Union's vast network of forced-labor camps.

KGB [kay-gee-**bee**]: **K**omitet **G**osudarstvennoi **B**ezopasnosti—the Committee for Government Security—the Soviet Union's dreaded secret police.

Manuscript [**man**-yoo-skript]: An author's writing, before it becomes printed as a book.

Moscow [**mah**-skoh]: The largest city of Russia, and its capital from 1389 until 1712, and again since 1918.

Nobel [no-**bel**] **Prize**: International prizes awarded each year to those who "have conferred the greatest benefit on mankind" through their outstanding achievement in the fields of physics, chemistry, medicine, literature, economics, and the promotion of peace. The award was established in 1895 by Alfred Nobel, the inventor of dynamite.

Petrograd [**peh**-troh-grad]: *see* **Saint Petersburg**.

Régime [ray-**zheem**]: A prevailing system of government, especially a repressive one.

Ricin [rye-sin]: a highly toxic poison, lethal even in tiny doses.

Russian Civil War: The war between the Whites and the Reds, from 1917 to 1922, that killed at least 5 million people and resulted in the establishment of a Communist state.

Russian Revolution: The February (1917) Revolution, when Tsar Nicholas II abdicated his throne, followed by a chaotic, violent summer, and then the October Revolution, when overnight the Communists seized power, which they held until 1991.

Saint Petersburg: The capital of Russia from 1712 until 1918, and the main setting of the Russian Revolution.

Samizdat [**sah**-miz-dot]: Self-published books and papers, made by hand and passed from person to person. Reading these could result in severe punishment from the Soviet government.

Sharashka [sha-**rosh**-ka]: A secret research-and-development laboratory that was an integral part of the Gulag system. Scientists and researchers sent to prison would frequently be forced to do research for the government in these facilities.

Soviet [**so**-vyet] **Union**: *see* **USSR**.

Thaw: From 1962 to 1964, the politics of the USSR were slightly relaxed. It was during this period that Aleksandr was able to publish *One Day in the Life of Ivan Denisovich*.

Town Meeting: A meeting open to voters of a town, who, together, make decisions about how the town is to be run. This is a common form of local government in Vermont and other New England states.

Treason [tree-zun]: The purposeful betrayal of one's country, usually to benefit another. Solzhenitsyn was falsely charged with treason in order to provide a plausible excuse for his expulsion.

USSR [yoo-es-es-**ar**]: **U**nion of **S**oviet **S**ocialist **R**epublics. The giant state that was formed after the Russian Revolution and the overthrow of the Tsars. At its zenith, it occupied one-sixth of the world's landmass, and was said to represent the coming triumph of Communism worldwide.

the **West**: The free countries of Western Europe, North America, and Asia Pacific, largely united by shared cultural values, political ideas ("free peoples, free markets") and a common Communist threat.

World War I: The war between the Triple Alliance and the Central Powers, from 1914 to 1918, that killed at least 30 million people and resulted in a drastic reconfiguration of the world order.

World War II: The war between the Allies and the Axis Powers, from 1939 to 1945, that killed at least 50 million people and set the table for the Cold War.

Zek [zeck]: Prisoner of the Gulag.

TIMELINE

1918 (December 11): Aleksandr Solzhenitsyn born in Kislovodsk, Russia. (His father, Isaaki, had died following a hunting accident in June 1918.)

1921: Taisia, Aleksandr's mother, goes to Rostov to find work as a typist. Aleksandr stays with his mother's family, then re-joins her in Rostov in 1925.

1930: Aleksandr's grandfather arrested and taken away.

1941: Aleksandr graduates Rostov University in Mathematics and Physics.

1941-1945: World War II. Aleksandr becomes an artillery captain and receives three medals for bravery.

1945 (February): Aleksandr is arrested for writing critical comments about Joseph Stalin in his private letters. He is sentenced to eight years in the labor camps (gulags), with permanent exile to follow at the completion of his prison term.

1947: Aleksandr is moved to a special prison, called a *sharashka*, where he is forced to do scientific research. Becomes the basis for his novel *In the First Circle*.

1950: Aleksandr is sent to a hard-labor camp where he works as a bricklayer. He later describes this experience in *One Day in the Life of Ivan Denisovich*.

1952: A surgeon in the Gulag removes Aleksandr's cancerous tumor.

1953: Aleksandr is exiled for life to Kok-Terek, Kazakhstan after completing his eight-year prison term. He teaches math and science in the local school. His cancer returns, and he is told that he has three weeks to live.

1954: Aleksandr is successfully treated with radiation therapy at a cancer clinic in Tashkent, Uzbekistan. This experience is the basis of *Cancer Ward*.

1956: The Soviet leadership changes, and Aleksandr is freed from exile. He teaches mathematics in high school.

1962: *One Day in the Life of Ivan Denisovich* is published in the Soviet Union.

1970: Aleksandr is awarded the Nobel Prize in literature, but fear of exile keeps him from receiving the prize in person. Aleksandr's first son, Yermolai, is born.

1972: Aleksandr's second son, Ignat, is born.

1973: In August the manuscript of *The Gulag Archipelago* is seized by the KGB; in December the first volume of *Gulag* is published in France. Aleksandr's third son, Stephan, is born.

1974: Aleksandr is arrested, deprived of his Soviet citizenship, and exiled from the USSR. He and his family settle in Switzerland.

1976: Aleksandr and his family move to Cavendish, Vermont, where he remains in exile until 1994. He writes *The Red Wheel*.

1989: *The Gulag Archipelago* is printed in the Soviet Union.

1991: The Soviet Union collapses.

1994: Aleksandr returns to Russia.

1995-1998: Aleksandr travels widely in the Russian provinces.

1997: Aleksandr is elected to the Russian Academy of Sciences.

1998: Aleksandr publishes the book *Russia in Collapse*; turns 80 years old; and attends the première of *Victory Celebrations* on the stage of the Taganka Theater.

2007: Russian Academy of Sciences votes Aleksandr a laureate of the Russian State Prize for "outstanding achievements in the field of humanities."

2008 (August 3): Aleksandr dies at his home in Moscow, Russia, age 89.

MAJOR WORKS

One Day in the Life Of Ivan Denisovich

Matryona's Home

Miniatures

In the First Circle

Cancer Ward

The Gulag Archipelago

The Red Wheel

The Trail

The Oak and The Calf

The Invisible Allies

Nobel Lecture

Harvard Address

когда я от Вас последний раз уез[жал]
[впечатле]ние, что в новом варианте Ваш[ей статьи есть]
некоторая непростота архитект[уры и]
[иску]сственность. Теперь я очень рад[остно вижу]
[чт]о этого нет, статья очень цель[ная, стройная]
[естест]венно - и естественны же для н[ас слова:]
"...": ведь это и есть Вы без грим[а, это]
[прям]ой мост через столетие.

Я воспользовался Вашим разреше[нием]
[внести] изменения прямо на деле ру[кописи]
это похоже на наглую правку, но [получилось ост]
рей и короче, раз уж мы не м[ожем иначе.]
Предложения Ваши я внес двумя ц[ветами]
[по] настоятельному желанию, темно-зелены[м и]
черным цветам пояснял 'на пол[ях' почему]
[дается] такое предложение. Эти послед[ние]
написаны понéволе мелковат[о, но надеюсь]
[так], что их достаточно будет Лю[ше чтобы]
[про]честь.

Ваше название мне очень нрави[тся, оно ох]
[ват]ывает всю тему статьи, доба[вить?]
[я п]редлагаю через точку, это хара[ктерно]
[сов]ременно и традиционнее - через [...]

Ещё я кое-где на полях поставил значки — это особое одобрение лучше по сравнению с письмами к Алигер).
Что ж, не называйте "Нового мира", отдельно напишите! (стр 2, я отме...

На стр 7 я не объяснил главного, вот что: на абзаце как будто уверенного выведения из какого-то вздору. И я предлагаю чуть смягч... вступиться за Герцена. Выбаву из Огарё... ать — ну, а много ли потеряли бы...
И самая последняя на страничке — "То - б - даже облегчивая и от неё?"

Для энергии окончания — и там уменить.

Ещё вот что удивительно: обвёл ли такой нагруженной мыслью стат... дел, статья легка! (Но не ...

Испалать же, Лидия Корнеевна думают! Статья готова, созрел...

Made in the USA
Lexington, KY
19 August 2018